The Sound Of Whales

A Play In One Act

by

David Charles MacLean

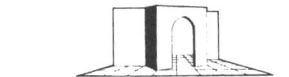

ANVIL PRESS PERFORMANCE SERIES

Copyright © 1996 by David Charles MacLean

All rights reserved. No part of this book may be reproduced by any means without the prior written permission of the publisher, with the exception of brief passages in reviews. Any request for photocopying or other reprographic copying of any part of this book must be directed in writing to the Canadian Reprography Collective (CANCOPY), 6 Adelaide Street East, Suite 900, Toronto, Ontario, Canada, M5C 1H6, 1-800-893-5777.

Cover design by JT Osborne

The Publisher gratefully acknowledges the assistance of the Cultural Services Branch, Ministry of Small Business, Tourism and Culture.

Printed and bound in Canada
First Edition

Canadian Cataloguing in Publication Data

MacLean, David C. (David Charles), 1952-
The sound of whales
(Anvil performance series, ISSN 1188-0872; no. 2)
ISBN 1-895636-10-8
I. Title. II. Series.
PS8575.L42S68 1996   C812'.54   C96-910381-6
PR9199.3.M331S68 1996

Represented in Canada by the Literary Press Group
Distributed by General Distribution Services

Anvil Press
175 East Broadway, Suite 204-A
Vancouver, BC
Canada   V5T 1W2
TEL: (604) 876.8710 FAX: (604) 879.2667

THE SOUND OF WHALES

FOREWORD by *Kim Selody*

I am very pleased that *The Sound of Whales* is being published. It was first read as a play at the Vancouver New Play Festival in 1994 and is one of David's strongest. It is the second time a play of his has been read at our Festival. *Samuel*, another emotionally gripping piece, was read the year previously. I knew David then as the man responsible for organizing all the cartoonists in the province to compile a book as a fundraiser for the Playwrights Theatre Centre (formerly the New Play Centre). But I soon found out what kind of playwright he was—talented, clear and driven. He was one of those playwrights who did not need to rely on our company to get his work produced.

When we read his play *Samuel*, some of the actors were confronted with an emotional journey that was extremely challenging, but which they knew instinctively to be true. Some people do not respond well to this kind of work, they feel it is too emotionally manipulative. But David has always struck me as the kind of playwright who tries to reach out, grab the audience by the heart and show it to them—right in front of their faces. This is true of *The Sound of Whales* and all of David's work.

In looking back through our library and archives, I came across several early drafts of David's work—an amazingly diverse collection of styles and ideas. It was as if in each case he was searching for the right concoction of style and content. I await with interest his next concoction.

Artistic Director
Playwrights Theatre Centre, Vancouver.

A DIRECTOR'S ANALYSIS

by Robert Garfat

The Sound of Whales is a lyric-comedy about language, our obsessive reliance upon it and how linear thought can inhibit understanding. It is a play about a man, Harry, who, while sitting in a park at the end of life, encounters horrifying and beautiful truths about the very nature of his existence.

Harry's drive is to understand. He has questions which are unanswered, largely regarding his relationship with his son. As he examines his inability to express through language the nature of his son's affliction, he moves toward a greater understanding of the limitations which a language-based society places upon the expression of personal experience.

Robert's drive is control. He is devoutly religious, with ardent Calvanistic morals and sensibilities, but while his self-proclaimed agenda is to save Harry, he will save himself first.

Nurse represents societal treatment of the aged. She cares for the physical and, to a degree, the psychological needs of her wards without adequately preparing them spiritually for their passage from this world.

Snake is a dweller of society's fringe. He is quite probably schizophrenic, eking out his meagre existence from the cast-offs of a society which denies his very existence. It is in Snake's final scene with Harry that we begin to understand the mythic implications of this character. As Snake frees Harry of the last vestiges of material existence, he assists Harry in making the transition to the fluid, ethereal realm beyond.

As Harry makes the journey from this world to the next,

the play moves from Naturalism to Imagism and the realistic form of the play's early scenes makes way for the looser, more allegorical aspects of the play's latter half.

The park setting for *The Sound of Whales* is at once urban —which is to say civilized and orderly—and 'wild' in the sense that nature is uncontrolled and in flux. The clearing is a place of meeting where the light of day pierces the shadowy canopy of leaves. It is Fall, and nature is winding the lively cycle down toward the cold season in preparation for future renewal and rebirth. As a whole, the setting represents the garden on the fringes of this material life, the gateway or no-man's-land between this world and the next. The park provides a perverse mirror of the mythological garden at the other end of man's existence, Eden.

The use of chorus in this play presents one with a whole set of directorial problems. The choreography of the chorus alone offers potent possibilities. Each encounter with the chorus propels Harry into new revelations, fresh perspectives from which to assess and continue his journey.

It would be a mistake to approach *The Sound of Whales* as a 'single issue' play. Certainly treatment of the 'differently abled' is an element of the script, but at its core the play is about Harry, his anger, his frustrations, his pain, and ultimately his salvation.

The Sound of Whales provides a contemporary corollary to *Everyman*. David MacLean's play has its roots in his personal experience in dealing with governmental, educational and medical bureaucracies. The frustration the playwright expresses toward these institutions is balanced by the love and devotion a father feels for his son. *The Sound of Whales* is at once tender and angry, intimate and universal.

Vancouver, BC, 1996.

PRELUDE

Choreographed and performed by Jan MacLean
Created in collaboration with Lighting Designer Rebecca Johnson

CHOREOGRAPHER'S NOTES

The Sound of Whales is filled with references to Harry's son, but at no point in the play does the son make an appearance. I was asked by the director to choreograph and perform *Prelude* in order to present the son's vision of the world. *Prelude* is a 10-minute movement piece that attempts to impart to the audience the experience of receptive and expressive aphasia.

The piece begins in darkness. The only sound is that of the dancer's feet repeating a rhythmical movement sequence. This sequence in darkness continues for a full minute, until gradually the lights come up and the audience sees a single dancer in a circle of light, surrounded by five chorus members. Each chorus member is situated beside a large rock and is softly reciting lines their character speaks in the play, the idea being that the audience knows the actors are speaking, but cannot make out what they are actually saying—very much like the condition of receptive aphasia. The gestures that the dancer performs are ritualistic in nature and incorporate American Sign Language. The sign "I need" builds through gesture until it can no longer be contained by the circle of light. At this point the light disappears and the voices of the chorus stop. There is complete darkness except for a single beam of light. The dancer explores the beam of light, playing with it, bouncing it, letting it wash over her, until she swallows it.

The circle of light reappears with the dancer again repeating the same signs/gestures, but her eye focus has now shifted out. Expression has become communication. The voices of the chorus resume, as the drone of a single bagpipe is heard. The voices and drone grow in volume as the dancer breaks out of the circle and performs a series of gestures/signs that attempt to communicate the frustration that the dancer/son is experiencing. The sequence grows in speed as the drone of the voices and bagpipe grows in volume. Finally the sequence falls apart and, slowly, with effort, a new sequence is put in place. Inner language has become outer language. The piece ends in blackout. The bagpipe drone builds to the opening of the play, acting as a bridge from the son's world to Harry's.

Jan MacLean, May, 1996.

Ed Astley and Paul Jarrett

The Sound of Whales was first produced by Dark Horse Theatre at the Firehall Arts Centre, Vancouver, BC in December, 1995. The production was directed by Robert Garfat with the following cast:

HARRY	Ken Kramer
ROBERT	Ed Astley
NURSE	Sue Astley
SNAKE	Paul Jarrett

Chorus

Ian Hand
Cheryl McNamara
Tracy Swaile
Meredith Vuchnich
Trevor White
Mariner Janes

Design: Rebekah Johnson, Jane Henry
Choreography: Jan MacLean
Stage Manager: Neil Scott

The Sound of Whales was first read at the Vancouver New Play Festival with the following cast:

HARRY	Duncan Fraser
ROBERT	Bill Sample
NURSE	Jaqueline Dandeneau
CHORUS	Don Thompson & Ann Warn Pegg

DEDICATION

This play is for my son, Danny.

Also for Roz and Jan who share the adventure.

CHARACTERS:

HARRY: In his early 70's

ROBERT: Roughly the same age as Harry

NURSE: A Pleasant woman in her 50's

SNAKE: A street person, any age, mentally volatile

CHORUS

1st DOCTOR: 30 (male or female)

2nd DOCTOR : Older (male or female but opposite gender of 1st Doctor)

ARTIST: Early 30's

SOCIAL WORKER: A woman in her 30's

PIG & DANCER: Gang members

A PIPE BAND: At least five women, from teenage years to early 20's, playing pipes and drums

In the BLACKOUT, *bagpipe* MUSIC *starts.* LIGHTS *come up to find a* PIPE BAND *of women upstage, playing and marching on the spot. The whole stage is covered with the leaves of autumn. A semi-circle of rocks span centre stage.* HARRY *and* ROBERT *are seated on two of the rocks. The* BAND *marches through the rocks.* HARRY *stands up and gestures after them as they walk upstage.*

HARRY: The sound of whales.

ROBERT: What?

HARRY: That sound, whales calling . . . that voice, you've heard it, you know what it means. A trial, Robert.

ROBERT: It's the wind. A storm.

HARRY: We're going to walk in the park. A trial on the trails.

ROBERT: We already went to the park.

HARRY: God, you're a fool. That was last week.

ROBERT: I lost track.

HARRY: I never lose track.

ROBERT: Yes you do. You can't tell who's alive or dead. You don't know if you're dead.

HARRY: *(points to a place on the floor near where he is sitting)* Look at this. It's the park. See. Trees, and a policeman on a horse, and a whale in the water. Look at that drawing there.

ROBERT: Where?

HARRY: My boy did this drawing.

ROBERT: I don't see anything.

HARRY: Look at it.

ROBERT: I can't see it.

HARRY: Get down.

ROBERT: There's no drawing down there.

HARRY: Kneel down. You like to kneel.

ROBERT: You should have put it on the wall.

HARRY: Come on, kneel.

ROBERT: No, I can see it now. Yes.

HARRY: No you can't.

ROBERT: Look, I'll bend closer.

HARRY: I thought you were my friend.

ROBERT: I can't do any more than this. I'm an old man. Okay, okay. See, I'm kneeling. Are you happy now?

HARRY: Look at the drawing.

ROBERT: I'm looking. This isn't a drawing.

HARRY: Yes it is.

ROBERT: It's the grain of the wood.

HARRY: My son.

ROBERT: You don't have a son.

HARRY: No son. She's thirty-six hours in labour, my wife. The baby's in distress. They get these forceps—they haul him out. The room has turned into glass. I say something stupid. "You bugger, it's about time." Stupid . . . and I laugh. I want to make everything all right. But he's being held by the nurse—doctors, experts, all useless now—and with his eyes he looks. I swear he looks at me and the eyes go inside forever. These black eyes look at me. I am the one that is naked. No son.

ROBERT: You're talking crazy again. The doctors should see you again. Where's the nurse?

HARRY: Then there was all that poop and pee stuff. Years of cute, you know. But he wouldn't talk. He said a word once and then it was gone. It disappeared and then was not said again. No. All the experts, they weren't so cute. Lord, experts. They didn't know .... My wife had a dream, she saw him looking up from under the water, trying to talk, his face under there, under the water, looking up .... And that follows me, that image. I can't even be haunted by my own dreams, I've got to be haunted by someone else's. What sort of man can't even have his own dreams?

ROBERT: A crazy asshole, that's who. I'm not sure, I might need to pee.

The NURSE *enters.*

NURSE: It's time for the little blue one and the pink one. What are you doing, Robert?

HARRY: He was trying to blow me again ... and he said the word asshole.

ROBERT: (*getting up from the kneeling position*) You're disgusting .... And ass-hole is two words.

NURSE: Now stop you two. I won't have this ...

HARRY: I don't want the pink one today.

NURSE: The pink one is especially good for you.

HARRY: I hate the pink ones.

> *The two men swallow their pills.*

ROBERT: I don't get a pink one. I never get a pink one.

NURSE: I hear that you grabbed Miss Ames' bottom again. Harry, no. Amie is a very nice girl, and it's only wishful thinking for you anyway. You're lucky that any of us put up with you. We're going to the park again, just like I promised. I'll be back in a minute and then we'll go to my car.

> *The* NURSE *exits.*

HARRY: The pink ones take your sex away.

ROBERT: What?

HARRY: Never mind, you're too old.

ROBERT: We went to the park already.

HARRY: That was last week. Go to the washroom.

ROBERT: I don't need to go to the washroom.

HARRY: Go to the washroom.

ROBERT: I don't feel like it.

HARRY: I don't want to be sitting there beside some old fart who wets himself. Queers in the woods, the horse police horsing, kids playing, the leaves blowing out to sea . . . and you walking around whining with your pants soaked.

ROBERT: That never happened. We're not going to the park because there's going to be a storm.

HARRY: Screw your storm. Do you hear that? Listen. A child can scream and when he's an old man he can suddenly hear it, his own howling.

ROBERT: I've got to go to the bathroom. Where's the nurse?

HARRY: You don't need the nurse, just undo your fly and pee right here.

ROBERT: You want to do something with her don't you? I know you do, but it isn't going to happen, Harry. I won't let it happen.

HARRY: Go on, pee in that flower pot over there.

ROBERT: Do you think I should?

HARRY: Absolutely.

ROBERT: I really need to go.

HARRY: Come on, man. Water that thing. I did it yesterday.

ROBERT: Someone could come in.

HARRY: No they won't. I'll watch. Come on man, mark some territory.

ROBERT *undoes his fly and pees in the flower pot.*

ROBERT: God, did I need to go.

HARRY: Nurse, Robert's peeing in the plant again.

ROBERT: *(hurries)* Damn you. I should know, I should know.

HARRY: You're old, you're just so goddamned old, how did you ever let yourself get so old? *(pause)* Do you hear that, that sound? *(pause)* Wind? Like a campfire. I'm not old. I can lie a thousand times just to hear the sound of the lie. It's become like music. I don't even know what the words of the lie mean anymore. I stayed separate watching them—everyone—huddled in nattering little groups deciding the most fearful thing to do, and then doing that thing. Every night I tell myself that I don't do that, not me . . . . My son . . . Central Aphasia they called it. No sound of longing against longing, just now this moment. He needs me, Robert.

ROBERT: You need more pills . . . . You know, this ramble thing. I should get the nurse.

ROBERT *exits.*

HARRY: *(as if unaware* ROBERT *has left)* We talk to ourselves and forget everything worth knowing. But my boy . . . . Angels sang to him . . . he could hear the music of God, Robert. He screamed one night—I don't know that he ever really slept. When I went in he was making sounds, the wind was talking. Somehow I could share his terror. It was a seizure. Flopping like a fish. I'm standing, helpless. Afterwards he said, I could hear the whales . . . he said that to me. And last night I saw them. They were horrible and marvelous . . . I was awake and asleep at the same time . . . alive and dead with the whales swimming next to me . . . in the room . . . my boy was one of them . . . looming black, gentle in the dark, the dance of water and blood, the black eyes of whales . . . .

The NURSE *enters.*

NURSE: Robert, where's he got to?

HARRY: Screwing the cat I think.

NURSE: Harry, Robert needs you to be nice to him. Why won't you just be nice to him?

HARRY: He peed in the planter again.

ROBERT *enters.*

ROBERT: I did not.

NURSE: Stop it you two. I'm doing this on my own you know, so I want you both to behave.

ROBERT: I went to the washroom.

HARRY: He'll wet himself again anyway.

NURSE: Good, good. Now, in the car.

All three of them sit as if they're in a car.

HARRY: My boy drew all the time.

NURSE: Yes, Harry.

ROBERT: We're going to the park aren't we?

NURSE: Every Thursday, Robert.

HARRY: I don't know how you stand him.

ROBERT: Last time we saw those girls.

NURSE: A pipe band. They were there for the Scottish dancers. Very nice.

ROBERT: Tartan. Red and black tartan. The sound was loud and . . . and the girls marched.

HARRY: He'd do a hundred drawings at a time. He was drawing genitalia on everybody when he was four. He did this perfect drawing . . . a man with two balls and a cock, just like that. It was extraordinary . . . breasts on women, dogs and cats with equipment. He understood at that age . . .

NURSE: Well, we know where he got his mind from, don't we Harry?

ROBERT: Your head is a black place, Harry. There's no room in it for the light. A dirty mind, full of noise.

NURSE: Robert, don't talk to Harry like that.

HARRY: He's mad at me because I won't go to church with him.

ROBERT: It could save you Harry. But no, not you, you'd rather dance with the devil.

HARRY: Fuck the devil.

NURSE: Really. In all my years I've never known any like you two. Now, we're here and I want none of your shenanigans.

The NURSE gets out of the car and comes around to help ROBERT out.

NURSE: Now look. You sit on the bench . . . yes, your favourite bench and I'll be back. I'm just going to the concession.

ROBERT: I want ice cream.

NURSE: We'll see. I'll be back soon.

The NURSE *exits.*

ROBERT: Where are the girls? You said they'd be here.

HARRY: Don't ruin this sunlight with your obsessions. The zoo's that way man, go stick your dick in the beaver.

ROBERT: I'm not listening you know. I'm going to enjoy today no matter what you do.

HARRY: Ducks. Did you bring the bread?

ROBERT: No. You were going to bring the bread. Look at those crows over there. They're dangerous.

The CHORUS *becomes crows.*

HARRY: They're not dangerous.

ROBERT: They're dangerous. They can kill you.

HARRY: Crows are our friends, Robert. They're black and evil and our friends. I love those crows.

ROBERT: Crows mean death.

HARRY: You know Robert, on the odd days when I don't want to kill you I quite like you. It's not easy to like someone who hates themself.

ROBERT: You're a very selfish talker Harry. I think that this day will go on whether you want to share it or not.

HARRY: I told you about my dream. I heard my boy calling me last night.

ROBERT: It's a sign of schizophrenia, hearing voices.

HARRY: But I'm disintegrating with style, don't you think?

ROBERT: The slave of action is the master of form. What we say matters. You think that it doesn't but it does.

HARRY: One of us is rambling, Robert, and I think it's you.

ROBERT: You know that I'm telling you the truth. I always tell the truth.

HARRY: I'm nervous. Today is . . . it's turning inside-out . . . can't you feel it?

ROBERT: Yes, yes I can feel it.

HARRY: He was four. He could barely speak at four. Some of it made sense. I got out of bed and there were drawings all over the walls. He drew this park. See where we are. I saw that tree over there. And he drew the sound of those birds. Animals, he loved animals. See that tree. He drew that tree. He called that 'Daddy's house.' That tree is my house . . . .

ROBERT: Why did he do that? Why draw things when they're already there?

HARRY grabs ROBERT by the collar.

HARRY: I'll kill you if you say stupid things like that. He needed to draw because he couldn't talk.

ROBERT: Right. He couldn't talk. Now let go.

HARRY: I mean he couldn't talk well.

ROBERT: He couldn't talk well. So kill me.

HARRY: I'm sorry. You're an old man, Robert. I hate old men.

ROBERT: Don't do that anymore. I hate that.

HARRY: You're just like all those goddamned doctors. They couldn't see him, they thought he was . . . well, they didn't know. They said there was no hope. It was congenital.

ROBERT: If the doctors said he was retarded then that means he was retarded.

HARRY: God help me I could kill you. He was not, you asshole. He drew, he drew everything.

ROBERT: Well, then he did.

HARRY: Things that don't exist. He made them exist.

ROBERT: I was only telling the truth.

HARRY: He saw more than me.

ROBERT: I always tell the truth.

HARRY: We want to talk. There's something in us that makes us talk. Everything was different for him. The light in the room. He could see what was going to happen next Tuesday. I didn't even know that anything was going on, anything at all. But now, I can hear those angels singing myself. The dream has stopped being a dream, Robert.

ROBERT: You always talk like you're trying to sell me something.

HARRY: And you talk as if court is in session. Everyone says the right thing, like it's their job to say the right fucking thing. They say the right thing at work and then they go home. They say the right thing at a party and then they go home. Say the wrong thing, and you're suddenly alone. For some reason a boy who has one foot in heaven threatens these people and they stop being people, they become machines.

ROBERT: Everything is being measured. All of our words, our time on this earth. My father preached a sermon once about a man who drank, who couldn't hold a job. The wife came to see my father. He said, "You must leave him, leave your husband." She looked at my father and said, "But I love him." I've been trying to figure out what it means. Did anyone ever love you like that?

HARRY: Yes. No.

ROBERT: No. Do you love anyone like that?

HARRY: I still have some things to do, Robert. I've got to find my boy.

ROBERT: Look. Some crumbs in my pocket. *(he throws them for the ducks)* The crows are coming instead. Get away crows.

HARRY: He could see inside the very soul of his mother. I was on the outside watching, mother and child. They were the same person. I couldn't tell where one stopped and the other began.

The crows become children playing airplanes, complete with SOUND EFFECTS. *They fly behind the men and form the following scene.*

MOTHER: Your father's going to take you for some tests. Be a good boy now. You can fly. You can fly on the bus. Let's see you now. Your haircut looks beautiful. The Greek barbers were sure you were a Greek boy because you look so adorable.

HARRY: They asked what language he was talking. It was jargoning. Words flowing like a river in the shop. It's his own language, I told them. "Yes," the barber said. Ten black hairs stretched over his bald head.

ROBERT: What?

HARRY: The barber's.

ROBERT: Oh.

MOTHER: Don't forget your jacket. Be sure to try your best.

The scene disperses with the birds as the CHORUS *exits.*

ROBERT: You know, I hope we don't see any of those Hari Krishna.

HARRY: The Hari-Crisco guys. They're all right. Hari-Crisco, Hari-Crisco. Crisco-Crisco, Hari-Hari.

ROBERT: You mock everyone.

HARRY: Now what does that make me, does that make me your friend?

ROBERT: Inside there's a meanness. I've always known that about you.

HARRY: I've got to take my son to the doctor's . . .

ROBERT: I don't understand why anyone likes you. I'm going to find Nurse.

HARRY: For the tests. They say they're important.

ROBERT: I'll tell her you hit me.

HARRY: I hit you?

ROBERT: Okay I won't, but don't do it again. Don't ever hit me again.

HARRY: Look, there he is.

ROBERT: What?

HARRY: I saw him.

ROBERT: Who?

HARRY: My son.

ROBERT: No.

HARRY: Down that trail. His red jacket. It was him.

ROBERT: Where are you going?

HARRY: I'll be back soon.

HARRY exits.

ROBERT: Wait. You're not supposed to.

SNAKE enters.

ROBERT: He shouldn't have left.

SNAKE: Who?

ROBERT: He'll get lost.

SNAKE: We're all lost, pal.

ROBERT: I can't find him, but I can save him.

SNAKE: Are you with that bible group?

ROBERT: Yes . . . and no.

SNAKE: I'd say no.

ROBERT: Then you'd be wrong. I don't know the group you're referring to but I know my bible and so I know them and they would know me. We're all together.

SNAKE: I know my bible and I can't figure them out at all. It's as if they're trying to protect God. As if God was some fragile thing. Personally I want protection from God.

ROBERT: You're insane.

SNAKE: Say what?

ROBERT: You're not really religious.

SNAKE: Come again there, pal.

ROBERT: You're one of the lost. Like my friend Harry.

SNAKE takes out a small knife.

SNAKE: I'm not lost, pal. Snake is my name and do you know what that means?

ROBERT: You're not scaring me.

SNAKE takes out an apple and slices it into 'boats'.

SNAKE: Well, the snake didn't leave the garden. No. Not me, pal. You think you're in with God, well he's not even offering anymore. The gate's rusted shut. You're out and I'm in. I see light in a way you can't even imagine. You don't know God because you're not terrified, man.

ROBERT: My mother used to cut them into boats like that.

SNAKE *offers an apple slice on the end of the knife.*
ROBERT *takes it.*

SNAKE: Those are nice shoes.

ROBERT: Thanks.

SNAKE: Do you need them?

ROBERT: What?

SNAKE: Are you going to be doing much walking? Looking for your friend.

ROBERT: No. I'm going to find him in here. *(hand on heart)*

SNAKE: Prayer.

ROBERT: Yes. He's close to being saved you know. If only he wasn't so stubborn. The reason he's so mean to me is that he's almost won over. He's afraid of salvation.

SNAKE: So your shoes are kind of up for grabs then?

ROBERT: You can't have my shoes. They're mine, I'm supposed to have them and you're not.

SNAKE: Have you noticed that we're the same size? Put that in your divine order, pal. That fact has meaning. And then this 'supposed to have' thing . . . your worthiness for shoes isn't all that apparent.

ROBERT: I know where I stand with God.

SNAKE: Don't I look like I deserve a good pair of shoes? You see these. Wrecked. Life, man. Life. I've been around the forest, battered in the service. I'm a walking testament.

ROBERT: Could I have another bit of apple?

SNAKE: *(giving him a piece off the knife)* Your friend?

ROBERT: Yes?

SNAKE: What shoe size is he?

ROBERT: We're the same. He borrowed a pair of mine today. He never looked after his shoes and now he borrows mine. And then he makes fun of me.

SNAKE: Which way did he go?

ROBERT: Always mocking. As if everything is a joke.

SNAKE: Was that him going in the trail a while back?

ROBERT: He acts as if I don't have appetites. As if I never undressed a woman. He acts as if I live in a fishbowl. Without feelings. It wasn't just him who lived. I did things, I laughed and sang. I had a whole life, a rich life.

SNAKE: Whoa! Easy. Here's the last piece of apple. Okay, do you have any change?

ROBERT: No.

SNAKE: I find that hard to believe.

ROBERT: I don't care what you believe.

SNAKE: And to think that I gave you my apple.

ROBERT: I'm sorry. Here.

Gives SNAKE *some change.*

SNAKE: Thank you. Now if you'll excuse me.

ROBERT: If I close my eyes I can see him.

SNAKE: You see him?

ROBERT: Yes.

SNAKE: Does he have any shoes?

ROBERT: He's in the water. Behind him there's a cross of fire.

SNAKE: Got it. Okay, see ya . . .

ROBERT: If you were a real snake you wouldn't need any shoes.

> SNAKE *exits quickly. The* NURSE *enters,* ROBERT *walks toward her.*

ROBERT: I want to see the monkeys.

NURSE: No, no, someone threw paper in their cage. It's not very neat; let's see the penguins.

> *The* NURSE *and* ROBERT *exit.*

> *The* CHORUS *become monkeys playing with paper. They then change into a maze of bustling paper bureaucrats which* HARRY *struggles through to meet the* 1ST DOCTOR. *The bureaucrats deliver the paperwork to the* 1ST DOCTOR *and exit.*

HARRY: Where's my boy?

1ST DOCTOR: He's in the other room playing. These test results prove that your son is mentally handicapped.

HARRY: Well of course, he can't talk . . .

1st Doctor: But he can't talk because he's . . . we think that he might eventually reach a mental age of ten.

Harry: No.

1st Doctor: It's best to accept it.

Harry: *(picking up leaves)* But these drawings . . .

1st Doctor: The tests show . . .

Harry: He can't talk, or hear exactly what you're saying, how the hell can he answer your goddamned questions?

1st Doctor: I know it's hard. But that's the point, he can't think because he has no language . . .

Harry: Not in words, but look at these pictures. He thinks in images. Every last goddamned thing you wanted to know in your tests is in these drawings.

1st Doctor: It's best if you accept it. After all there's nothing wrong with being mentally handicapped.

Harry: Of course there isn't. You're retarded and I accept you . . .

1st Doctor: You have trouble controlling your anger, don't you? I worry that it might constitute a danger to your son. I shall have a talk with Social Services. They'll be in touch. Soon.

The 1st DOCTOR *exits, handing the paperwork to the* SOCIAL WORKER *on his way.*

Harry: This tree is my house, isn't it son? That one is your sister's, and that's your mother's . . .

The SOCIAL WORKER *enters.*

SOCIAL WORKER: It must be hard having a boy like that.

HARRY: This is my house. My boy gave me this house.

SOCIAL WORKER: You must get angry.

HARRY: God, yes.

SOCIAL WORKER: Do you beat him?

HARRY: I should love to beat someone. At school five bullies made a ring around him, taunting him. Say spit, they said. When he did they mimicked him. They laughed, then they beat him. It's best that I accept it. He'll have to learn, the principal said. Accept it. Accept *what* for christ's sake. They have no fucking idea, they have no fucking idea what they're saying. I look for the bullies and they're just kids. Kids. I talk and the right thing is said, or the wrong thing, and we feel better or worse and something magical is happening in the next room with my son. He's playing. I should love to beat someone, to grab them and say, Listen to this story, it's the story of someone who is larger than this world. My boy is under water. Can you help him?

SOCIAL WORKER: I see. A boy in heaven, a father in hell?

HARRY: Am I the real enemy?

SOCIAL WORKER: You are not a simple man are you? I'm not sure . . . your version is just so different from the doctor's. Any trouble and we seize the boy. The file is in the hands of the proper authorities. We'll be in touch.

The SOCIAL WORKER *gathers papers together,*
closes briefcase. Starts toward door.

HARRY: Proper authority? *(shouts)* There is no *proper authority.*

The SOCIAL WORKER *exits.*
There is the SOUND *of a phone ringing.*

MISS FIBS: Hello, this is Miss Fibs from the Special Learning Daycare. I need to talk to the father . . .

HARRY: Yes, that's me.

MISS FIBS: I'd like to set up a meeting.

HARRY: It's about my son . . .

MISS FIBS: He's been hitting the other children . . .

HARRY: Of course he has.

MISS FIBS: I'm sorry you take that attitude.

HARRY: You've kept him at the same level. He's bored. You said you'd put him ahead.

MISS FIBS: Our tests show . . . . We're up on the latest literature on the subject and we've kept him back, well, because he hasn't gone through all the stages . . .

HARRY: You lied to us.

MISS FIBS: The parents often don't understand . . .

HARRY: And now he's bored and angry. He knows that you think he's stupid and so he's becoming a thug. You're turning my son into a thug. Why the hell won't any of you people ever listen . . .

MISS FIBS: If you can't be reasonable . . .

HARRY: You're lowering your expectations of his intelligence to his expressive level. You view the world through the window of language . . . . He does not. In some ways he's much smarter than either of us . . .

MISS FIBS: I think that's enough. I'm going to recommend that your son be placed in a class that specializes in behaviour problems . . .

HARRY: No, don't do that.

MISS FIBS: It's all right. I often have to deal with hostile parents. I can handle it, believe me. Goodbye.

HARRY: It's not going to happen that way because it can't happen that way, Miss Fibs.

HARRY *exits. The* NURSE *enters with* ROBERT.

NURSE: Harry, it's time for your medicine. Harry where are you?

ROBERT: Gone and good riddance . . .

NURSE: If you don't behave we'll go right now.

ROBERT: No.

NURSE: Don't *no* me Robert, not now.

ROBERT: I want you to take me to the Australian part.

NURSE: I don't have time, Robert . . .

ROBERT: For his own sake we have to leave him here.

NURSE: What?

ROBERT: I was thinking about Harry, how to help him.

NURSE: I've become nervous again. I hate it when I get nervous.

ROBERT: I want to go to the Australian exhibit.

NURSE: Robert, can't you please, just this once, go by yourself. If I don't see you there later we'll meet back here at four.

ROBERT: We always meet here.

NURSE: Yes, we do.

ROBERT: I could find him you know. He's chasing those girls in the band. I could find him. Or I could go to the Australian exhibit.

NURSE: Robert, I have to sit down. I really don't feel very well.

ROBERT *exits.* SNAKE *enters and overhears the* NURSE.

NURSE: *(searching)* It's all poop and pee, first the babies and now the old men. The human body is so disappointing. Harry you get back here right now . . . I'll miss my hair appointment, Harry; so you just get back here.

SNAKE: I saw him you know.

NURSE: What?

SNAKE: Your friend.

NURSE: Harry?

SNAKE: He's fine.

NURSE: You've seen Harry?

SNAKE: Yes, of course. I met the other one too.

NURSE: Robert.

SNAKE: He was telling me how he wants new shoes.

NURSE: Where's Harry now?

SNAKE: He was playing a game on you. Hiding.

NURSE: I hate it when he does that.

SNAKE: He'll come back soon. I think he's in the can now.

NURSE: Sometimes I could—well, I don't know.

SNAKE: It can wear you down.

NURSE: What?

SNAKE: Looking after people.

NURSE: Those two . . .

SNAKE: Do you love them?

NURSE: What? I don't know. Really, what a question.

SNAKE: You remind me of someone.

NURSE: And just who do I remind you of?

SNAKE: My mother actually.

NURSE: Young man, I am not your mother.

SNAKE: None other.

NURSE: What?

SNAKE: I said that you had beautiful hair.

NURSE: I was going to get it done today.

SNAKE: You should.

NURSE: Does it look that bad?

SNAKE: Not at all. But looking after other people . . . I don't know, it can leave a gap.

NURSE: It can.

SNAKE: You lose track of where they stop and you begin.

NURSE: You do.

SNAKE: You need a moment.

NURSE: What?

SNAKE: A moment. I can tell. With people fussing over you. What, what's wrong?

NURSE: I don't know.

SNAKE: You'd feel guilty, wouldn't you?

NURSE: A bit. Yes.

SNAKE: Just getting your hair done.

NURSE: I'm with my boys.

SNAKE: They'll be fine. They're allowed on their own aren't they?

NURSE: Well, yes, for a time.

SNAKE: There you are. You see.

NURSE: You appear to know a great deal about me.

SNAKE: You're like my Mom. Almost the same person.

NURSE: Have you ever looked after anyone Mr . . . ?

SNAKE: No, never, not even myself usually.

NURSE: You don't look . . .

SNAKE: What?

NURSE: Nothing. Sorry.

SNAKE: Sorry and nothing do not go together. You looked at me and you suddenly realized that I'd slept in my clothes. And you're right, I have. Yes.

NURSE: That's fine.

SNAKE: No it's not. That is not fine with you. If you were really my mother that never would've happened, now would it?

NURSE: This is a strange conversation. How did we get on to mothers?

SNAKE: My mother's dead.

NURSE: What?

SNAKE: Last week. It was sudden. Over there. She fell over, just fell over.

NURSE: I'm sorry. Really.

SNAKE: I haven't been myself. I look a mess I know. I'm sorry . . .

NURSE: No, no, no. I'm so sorry.

SNAKE: And then I saw you and . . . I've been rambling haven't I . . .

NURSE: No, it's fine really. Have an apple. *(takes an apple from her handbag)* Is there anything I can do?

SNAKE: I'd like to just sit.

NURSE: Of course. Do you have any other family?

SNAKE: No. And you?

NURSE: A sister.

SNAKE: I wish I had a sister.

NURSE: I haven't seen her in years.

SNAKE: But you were close.

NURSE: Well, yes and no.

SNAKE: Did you love her?

NURSE: Well, yes. My sister used to cry, almost all the time. She's married now.

SNAKE: Married, but probably still crying. That would be my guess.

NURSE: Maybe she got through to something.

SNAKE: New shoes, a new look, different weather. Anything is possible.

NURSE: I mean, did she come to grips in a certain way, with certain things?

SNAKE: Please tell me exactly what you mean. I hate to admit it but I'm confused.

NURSE: Life. Did she discover how to live her life? Is that what happened?

SNAKE: I'd have to say yes. I just see a big yes in the sky and so that's the answer I'm going to give. Yes, she did.

NURSE: Everyone liked me the best, or at least I thought they did. I couldn't help thinking that she was off . . . I don't know. . . doing things. Seeing people, real people, not like the people I met. People that wanted something from me. Helpless people, sick people. I kept thinking that somehow she knew real people, and that she kept them hidden from me. Was she doing that, I used to wonder.

SNAKE: She was.

NURSE: Please don't make fun of me.

SNAKE: No, no, no. *(pause)* What is your name?

NURSE: Helen.

SNAKE: You must believe, Helen, that I would never do that. Sometimes I wonder what I've said, I see this effect and I realize I've said something. But in your case Helen I just can't help feeling that I know you.

NURSE: You know me?

SNAKE: I know about you. People need you. It has become your life.

NURSE: It matters.

SNAKE: Yes. You brought your friends to this park. It was the right thing to do.

NURSE: I'm good . . . very good to my boys . . .

SNAKE: And they love you for it. You must promise me one thing.

NURSE: What?

SNAKE: That you'll get your hair done.

NURSE: I couldn't. I've missed my appointment.

SNAKE: Not if you hurry.

NURSE: My boys . . .

SNAKE: I'll keep an eye on them. Go. You'll be back in half an hour. We'll be fine.

NURSE: I'm being silly. I've often left them for an hour or more. I don't know why I'm so skittish today.

SNAKE: Because it's the day of days. Helen, I'll check on your friends. Goodbye.

ROBERT *enters through the* CHORUS. *The* CHORUS *becomes a sensuous mass of lovers making out in slow motion.* ROBERT *stumbles by this, moving in normal time, both drawn to and appalled by the spectacle.*

ROBERT: I'm sure he's followed those girls in the band. They must be swimming nude in the duck pond and he's watching them. He hid behind the trees and watched them undress and now he's giggling and squirming like some stupid fish as they swim with their bare asses and breasts gleaming in the sun . . . *(shouts)* Damn you Harry! You leave those girls alone. They don't want you. *(weeping)* They don't want you, do you hear!

ROBERT exits as HARRY enters.

ROBERT: For God's sake just let him die. People have to die you know.

HARRY: I can't think. I just can't think anymore. Last night I dreamed that my dink fell off. Damn those pink pills . . .

HARRY enters an area where an ARTIST is painting.

ARTIST: You're standing right in front of what I'm drawing.

HARRY: Someone should be punished.

ARTIST: You have an interesting face. Middle European.

HARRY: I was looking for my son. He did thousands of drawings. They didn't understand.

The ARTIST starts to sketch HARRY.

ARTIST: They?

HARRY: All of them.

ARTIST: Ah yes, society. How convenient for you; society is to blame. Why don't you blame artists? We're used to it.

HARRY: That drawing you have there.

ARTIST: Hold still, please. Now turn a bit. Not many faces like that. Where did you get those bones?

HARRY: Do you know where my boy is?

ARTIST: Yes. Now I have something you want. God I love that. Have you noticed how life is never boring when you have something that someone else wants.

HARRY: Please, where is he?

ARTIST: Hold still. I can talk as I work. It relaxes me, as long as I lead the conversation.

HARRY: Was he all right?

ARTIST: Who?

HARRY: My son.

ARTIST: Just a minute.

HARRY: Where is he?

ARTIST: I've got to do this bit again. I tell my students, the difference between being a good artist and a great artist is a willingness to scrape off the paint and start again. Tell me, was he an artist?

HARRY: Who?

ARTIST: Your son.

HARRY: I don't know.

ARTIST: You don't know?

HARRY: I don't know.

ARTIST: How could you not know? It's the most important thing in the world. All of this shit will fall into the sea. All of the cars will rust, the houses rot. The only thing that can last is the image that rides on God's wind. Nothing else can do it. Everyone is so pathetically stupid and unaware that I get quite depressed sometimes. Except for your son. Your son is probably one of the special ones. Did you see that? Did you support him? Did you let him know that colour is all and form is the refuse of mystery? Well, did you?

HARRY: Yes. No. I knew something was happening but . . .

ARTIST: You don't know?

HARRY: I don't know.

ARTIST: Damn you.

HARRY: Damn me.

ARTIST: I hate being witness to such bone-headed stupidity. Probably the only problem your son had was you.

HARRY: Please stop it.

ARTIST: No, my friend, it's you who are on trial. You are the one who did not do . . .

HARRY: No. I did. I tried.

ARTIST: You did nothing.

HARRY: You're insane.

ARTIST: I wish I *was* insane. It makes your work catch on fire. What do you think?

Shows portrait to HARRY.

HARRY: My boy. Where is he?

ARTIST: Did it ever occur to you that I could be your son? Did it?

HARRY: No, not you.

Artist: The light is speaking in a language you do not understand. Lord, why do I waste my time . . . *(Harry grabs the artist who pulls away).* I saw him. He touched me on the shoulder, and there was something so calming about him. I drew him quickly afraid that he might leave . . . . You know, he never said a word. Not one word. And then he left.

ARTIST *exits. The* CHORUS *turns its back, then turns around slowly, depicting a corporate scene.*

HARRY: I need some time off work. We've got to go and see another stupid doctor.

BOSS: Harry, we're missing fifteen IBM typewriters.

HARRY: All the doctors do is talk . . . . What if we couldn't talk I ask them, if we could only think in pictures, like my son does. Do you understand? I'm talking about my boy. He's somewhere. Do you know what I mean? He just isn't here. Not all the time.

BOSS: The detectives think that someone at night simply took them out the side door and put them in the trunk of their car . . .

HARRY: I could teach him sign language. I'd need to change my hours, just shift them . . .

BOSS: Probably took three nights to steal the lot. We didn't notice because they were in the storage room . . .

HARRY: So someone else could handle the first map . . .

BOSS: Harry, you type don't you?

HARRY: What?

BOSS: You type?

HARRY: Yes.

BOSS: You don't need to?

HARRY: No.

BOSS: But you do?

HARRY: Yes.

BOSS: A very esoteric crime don't you think?

HARRY: What?

BOSS: Typewriters are all-but-useless now. This is the age of computers, Harry. Our nervous system has been extended throughout the world, into space itself. It interests me.

HARRY: Yes.

BOSS: A clever, useless crime. Poof. All of us typing away, but to some purpose of course. The person who committed this crime does not know his own purpose. Do you follow me?

HARRY: My boy draws, all the time. When we're out he wants us to go home so that he can draw what he's seen.

BOSS: Show me your hands.

HARRY: What?

BOSS: Yes, I'm interested in hands. There, see that line . . . Harry, I'm shocked. Really.

HARRY: What?

BOSS: I want you to know that I'm very empathetic, that I understand. A mind like yours intrigues me. But here Harry we must handle the weather. The weather, as you know, is very, very large.

HARRY: Yes, yes it is.

BOSS: You do know don't you Harry?

HARRY: What?

BOSS: That I understand.

HARRY: Oh yes.

BOSS: Good. You can pick up your cheque tomorrow. There will be three months severance on it.

HARRY: What?

BOSS: Yes, I know it's generous. Now if you don't mind . . .

HARRY: No, no . . .

BOSS: Harry, don't make this harder than it has to be. We're both men, with blood in our veins. None of this is lost on me . . .

HARRY: I did nearly everything for the company . . . for you . . .

BOSS: Of course you did . . .

HARRY: I need to help my boy . . .

BOSS: Your boy. Good heavens, by all means help your boy.

The CHORUS *transforms into a gang. The character of* DANCER *talks as if the scene is a rap song and he has a harmonica that he uses periodically.*

PIG: Hey you, old guy.

DANCER *starts clapping slowly.*

HARRY: No.

PIG: No, as in what?

DANCER: To be or to be not man.

HARRY: I don't remember meeting you.

PIG: There you go getting negative, and we haven't even met. Who are you?

HARRY: Harry.

PIG: They call me Pig, but I think it would be a mistake if you called me Pig. I might have to kill you. *(laughs)*

HARRY: I used to remember . . . things.

PIG: I can guarantee you'll remember me.

HARRY: I remember the light on my hands as my wife wept.

DANCER: Yeah, light. That's cool. Keep it goin' man.

PIG: You got any money?

HARRY: My son ran away.

DANCER: That's cool too.
  (Beat)
  Like away and gone
  (Beat)
  Like a black hole in time
  Man, I gotta think about that.

PIG: Yeah, okay, we do it the hard way. Hey, Jack, are we secure here? Keep a look-out okay?

Pushes HARRY.

PIG: Did I push you? I'm so clumsy.

HARRY: He was in the old cement works one day. They'd tumbled down.

PIG: You don't say.

HARRY: We talked. I talked and the light poured from his heart.

PIG: Very nice. You talked with your son.

HARRY: Just me. Only I spoke.

PIG: Did your son have any money?

HARRY: No one knows where the short-term memory resides, what part of the brain.

PIG: You want to fun the pig. Old guy words. Tell me that brain stuff again.

HARRY: If you don't have a short-term memory you can't speak . . .

PIG *hits* HARRY *in the stomach.*

HARRY: . . . except by a great effort of will.

PIG: Really. Do keep on, I want to know this stuff . . .

Hits HARRY *again.*

PIG: . . . really I do.

HARRY: At least five things in our short-term memory in order to speak.

DANCER: Cool. Five things, five things
(Beat)
Five an' five an' five man
(Beat)

PIG: You might have noticed that I'm talking to you.

HARRY: No one knows where their memory is . . .

PIG: Words coming out of my mouth.

DANCER: Rain through your brain. *(blows into harmonica)*

PIG: Now you tell me what I'm talking about okay?

HARRY: Something broken, thoughts can't get out. A connection, not words . . . but light.

DANCER: Memory is in the money, man.

PIG: Hey, we got a doctor here. Hey doc, I got one big question. Do I seem like a wolf to you? Well?

HARRY: Wolf.

PIG: You got it.

HARRY: The teeth are light.

DANCER: We could free you
(Beat)
Got the right light man
The sin behind your teeth
(Beat)
Keep goin', Doc

HARRY: Not a doctor. You can't fix people.

PIG: I can fix people.

Shoves HARRY *from member to member as* DANCER *recites.*

DANCER: Memory bleeds along the road
    On coins of red and gold
    Ripper come on come on the right
    Does the red dance all night
    Don't talk don't talk just pray
    Sweet baby is blue honey all day

PIG: Come on old man, let's see the green.

> HARRY *turns his pockets inside-out.*
> *A few coins and bills fall to the ground.*

HARRY: There. That's money.

PIG: Bad shit here.

DANCER: Disrespect to the Wolf.

PIG: And you appeared to be such a nice old man.

GANG MEMBER: He don't like you Pig.

PIG: I guess we gotta do the dirge rap.

DANCER: And the litany of pain, man, don't forget the litany of pain.

PIG: Okay. I was trying to explain something here. Do you believe that there is such a thing as a wolf among us? Let's say a wolf in the water. You know with that memory bit, I can see that, that was cool. But the travelling killer whale, the transient whale, does not speak lest he be heard. *Lest he be heard.* Do you understand that silence? Only the weak make noise, man. Have you ever thought that the silence could be a code?

And that code states that I don't bend down for money. Do you want me to stoop down and pick that up? Is that what you want? Huh? No answer. There you go being all negative again.

GANG MEMBER: He's got the big-time mouth, Pig.

PIG: Pick it up, or we'll do the red dance old man. And when you hand it to me you tell me my name.

Pushes HARRY. *The* CHORUS *members trade off lines.*

DANCER/GANG: Transient black oh so cool
    Whisper and swim whisper and swim

PIG: And you damn well better get it right.

DANCER/GANG: An' the seal man don't see him
    Don't hear him, it's already done in

PIG: My name old guy. Is it Pig? Can you say that?

DANCER/GANG: Killer in water eats warm tonight
    In and out, sealed up tight
    It's cool it's cool the song unspoken
    The rules unbroken, asshole

PIG: Come on old man, my name.

HARRY *appears to be experiencing chest pain.*
He hands the money to PIG.

DANCER/GANG: Eat the bread an' drink the blood
    Words from Christ on the wall
    Slow-mo bleed and we're kind
    Asshole

PIG *pockets the money.*

PIG: Now you tell me my name, tell me my fucking name.

PIG *grabs* HARRY, *eyeball to eyeball, contemplating definitive violence. Throws* HARRY *down. The* GANG *exits.* HARRY *lies still for a moment.*

HARRY: I had sex with Mary and Jane and Lisa. In and out . . .

LISA: Harry, Harry, oh Harry.

HARRY: You're beautiful . . .

LISA: I'm beautiful . . .

HARRY: God, you're beautiful . . .

LISA: Oh God . . .

HARRY: Oh God . . .

LISA: Oh . . .

HARRY: Oh . . . I've forgotten something . . .

LISA: What?

HARRY: Where's Mary?

LISA: Bastard.

HARRY: Where's Jane?

LISA: Fuck off, Harry . . .

HARRY: No, I need you. I need you all. I called to you yesterday, and the day before. You're so beautiful.

CHORUS: Fuck
Off
Harry

CHORUS *exits*. HARRY *rises*.

HARRY: I'm waiting by my tree. I'll just be waiting here.

1ST DOCTOR *enters*.

1ST DOCTOR: Oh hello, I'm glad I ran into you. The results of the EEG are in and they're very, um, unusual. At the back of the brain, the anterior region, the scan reveals that your son has very large theta and delta waves. A ratio of 5 to 1. These are the wavelengths associated with deep sleep and . . . um, the subconscious. Less than one in a hundred-thousand have this pattern. You were right, our tests were far too limited. Your son is dreaming, always asleep. These large delta and theta waves washing over his conscious mind . . . um . . . he is . . . a *god* of sorts. But, of course, I mean he sees . . . well, the impulsive behaviour is not really . . . um . . . . In my forty years of neurology I've never seen anything . . . seen anyone quite . . .

The MOTHER *enters*.

MOTHER: . . . as beautiful. A wave washes over him. Harry, I've put all of his drawings in the closet. There are thousands of them. I know you want to save them, but what does it mean? We'll have to do something about all of this clutter.

1ST DOCTOR: The mystery is beyond all of us at this point.

HARRY: That's not good enough.

1ST DOCTOR: There is nowhere else to go, we're done.

HARRY: We've got to fix it.

1ST DOCTOR: Are you a religious man? Yes, really pray. Use the hospital chapel. It will help.

1ST DOCTOR exits. ROBERT enters.

HARRY: God. God, you son-of-a-bitch you help my son right now, right fucking now. Do you understand you asshole? You help him right now, right now. *(drops to his knees)* My boy, my poor little boy. He can't talk, for christ's sake he can't talk. I did all the stupid stuff. My life goes by, just goes by . . . but you help my boy. He's under the water. You get down here and you do something, you help him to talk. Do you hear me? You help him to . . . he shouldn't have to . . . he needs . . .

The BAND marches across the stage.

ROBERT: It's not right to call God an asshole. You've been struck down haven't you?

HARRY: His eyes. He was a fucking angel.

ROBERT: You can't say that about angels.

HARRY: I'm in the woods.

ROBERT: You're in the woods.

HARRY: I'm dying.

ROBERT: I'll save you from hell, Harry.

HARRY: Please stop being afraid of everything. *Look at me.*

ROBERT: I don't want to see evil things. I've done the right thing all my life and it has to matter. It does matter. You won't listen but you can't stop me praying for you.

HARRY: I'm going under the water. I'm afraid . . . I'm afraid for christ's sake.

ROBERT: They always loved you. Their eyes are different when they look at you. You've never done the right thing and you're always seen. I hardly exist when I'm around you, Harry. I hate you but I'm going to change that. I'll pray and it will be all right.

HARRY: I'm sick, Robert.

ROBERT: Yes.

HARRY: I don't want to die . . .

ROBERT: I knew what you wanted to do to those girls. You're always saying things that get people upset. God had a place for you Harry and you didn't want to be in that place. You always wanted to cause trouble. To be noticed. God humbles those that scream at him, Harry.

HARRY: The angels are right here Robert, they are in front of us all of the fucking time. Your precious heaven has been right in front of you all your life and you can't see it, you've never seen it. It's the people we hate that can help us the most, but we must stop hating them. I'm trying to not hate you.

ROBERT: When you see your son he will be bathed in light.

HARRY: Robert, I don't like being alone with this.

ROBERT: You'll ruin yourself, you always do. I make you pure and you go and ruin it again. I'll pray for you. I will. You'll be saved. You will. I promise.

HARRY: Robert.

ROBERT: Yes.

HARRY: I'm sorry. I treated you like the black side of myself.

ROBERT kisses him on the cheek.

ROBERT: Goodbye, Harry. Don't say anything. You'll ruin yourself.

ROBERT goes to another part of the stage.

HARRY: Robert. Rob. Help me. Please.

NURSE enters, ROBERT intercepts her.

NURSE: Robert, where were you?

ROBERT: I was looking for Harry.

NURSE: Did you see him?

ROBERT: We should go. Harry is lost.

NURSE: We can't just leave him . . . . The storm is almost here.

ROBERT: Harry is salt.

NURSE: You should be ashamed of saying that about Harry. He's your best friend. We've got to find him. Robert, what can we do? We'll find him. We shouldn't have come here. There's such a wind.

ROBERT: I want to go home.

NURSE: Well we can't go home until we find Harry. He needs his pills.

ROBERT: He's probably dead by now.

NURSE: Don't say that . . .

ROBERT: People die you know.

NURSE: I know people die, I'm a nurse. If he doesn't have his medicine . . . I don't know. We have to go for help, Robert.

ROBERT: I'd like some more ice cream on the way back.

NURSE: Robert, stop it. Maybe he's at the car. Come on . . .

2ND DOCTOR enters.

2ND DOCTOR: There's been a mistake. Someone gave me your son's file by mistake. It's filled with . . .

HARRY: *(holding leaves)* Letters. I've written dozens of letters, over a hundred pages *(throwing leaves in the air)*. No one even read the damned things.

2ND DOCTOR: About your son. Yes, and the drawings appear to be . . .

HARRY: Better things, things you can't even test, but you were too stupid to see . . .

2ND DOCTOR: Of course we were. The drawings show function. But his language . . .

HARRY: He has his own language. It's like whales talking at each other through those trenches. Sending messages around the world.

2ND DOCTOR: Of course he does. It's too bad there were no whales on his test.

HARRY: It was wrong.

2ND DOCTOR: Of course it was wrong. But really Harry, your son, you couldn't change him so now you're off changing the world. It hasn't gone all that well, has it Harry?

HARRY: They said he was mentally retarded.

2ND DOCTOR: Any fool will tell you he's mentally retarded. Do you listen to fools?

HARRY: I wanted you to save him.

2ND DOCTOR: Do you understand the results of the tests?

HARRY: Yes.

2ND DOCTOR: Do you love him?

HARRY: Yes.

2ND DOCTOR: Then you saved him. Trust in nature, Harry.

2ND DOCTOR exits. The NOISE of crows completely overwhelms the scene, as does the SOUND of wind. The CHORUS covers HARRY in leaves. SNAKE enters and trips over HARRY.

SNAKE: Don't you fuck with me, pal. You don't ever fuck with me. Are we clear on that? Good. You got an apple? I have one. You want it?

HARRY: Thank you.

SNAKE: Not so fast.

HARRY: Sorry, I didn't mean to be fast.

SNAKE: Yeah, well it can happen. Right?

HARRY: I'm lost.

SNAKE: You got anything, pal? A little more change here. *(pause)* I said, do you have anything *(pulls HARRY to his feet)*. Oh well, we can get to that. That's it, I sit and you walk. Could you please stop shuffling like that. Hey, don't you stare at me, pal. See these eyes. These eyes and I have some secret that is mine. Not yours pal, mine.

HARRY: Have you seen my son?

SNAKE: Maybe. Yeah. I know the guy.

HARRY: Where is he?

SNAKE: I'm thinking.

HARRY: Yes.

SNAKE: Hey, this could take a while.

HARRY: My son is special.

SNAKE: Then I know him. He said something to me just yesterday.

HARRY: What was it?

SNAKE: I'm thinking. I can't remember.

HARRY: Please.

SNAKE: Hey, let's cut the pressure here. Christ I hate that.

HARRY: I'm sorry.

SNAKE: I'll remember. They were important words. Not like the words we've said here. Don't you just hate it when you realize that you've said something small. Trivial.

HARRY: Yes, I hate that.

SNAKE: Are you mocking me? Because if you're mocking me I know a place where old men can still sing . . .

SNAKE spears the apple with his pen knife.

HARRY: I hate small talk. You know, when there's nothing in the queue . . .

SNAKE: Nothing waiting and you're caught.

HARRY: Yes.

SNAKE: Well, you've seen me talk small.

HARRY: No.

SNAKE: Some of the words back there were small.

HARRY: I didn't notice.

SNAKE: Good. Something on your mind?

HARRY: My son.

SNAKE: You look tired. Lie down. I'll take care of everything. Come on now . . .

SNAKE helps HARRY off with his jacket, going through the pockets as he talks.

Are you here with that bible group? One of the ministers? Did you bring a lunch? (HARRY *points*) A candy bar. Very nice. Seen God around? No. I gave him what-for the other day. You know how he keeps getting the context wrong. Not to mention the peaks and valleys. Gave him what-for. Didn't tell him to fuck off though. You don't tell God to fuck off. That is impolite. Do you know your bible? Probably not. I'm working on a new version. It's all up here.

I don't like the beginning they have. In the beginning was The Word. How dare the beginning start with something as insubstantial as a word. What if the word was made flesh and the flesh never learned the words. What if the flesh didn't know that there was some God somewhere giving dictation.

Maybe we're putting up bits of acoustic dust, making mirrors of noise. Just that. What the hell is a word anyway? Infidel or house guest? Both? Or maybe just something to keep you from noticing.

Whirls HARRY's *jacket like a bullfighting cape. He pockets some bills he's found in the pocket, and drops the jacket on* HARRY.

The scratch and sniff of the pack will fill you in, buddy. Trust that. Just head back into the woods there. Leave me your boots maybe.

LIGHTS: *Lightning, faintly in the distance.*

HARRY: Did you see that?

SNAKE: What if the worst things about us are the best? What if God doesn't watch over us, how horrible. What if He does? How could I stand that. These word things are the tools. Why do I assume that God uses the same tools? Some days God is a woman. That scares me you know.

HARRY: Me too.

SNAKE: Someone was nice to me once. I mean *really* nice, like for no real reason. Scared the hell out of me. I thought that my skin was going to fall off. All of me was going to spill into the world. When God's like a woman I feel like that and I run. Have you been listening to any of this?

HARRY: Yes.

SNAKE: Then what did I say?

HARRY: You're frightened.

SNAKE: Fuck you. I thought I told you not to fuck with me. You know the snake never had to leave the Garden of Eden, pal. No, he didn't.

HARRY: No.

SNAKE: And just who the hell do you think you're talking to?

HARRY: Have you seen my son?

SNAKE: Yes I have.

HARRY: Where is he? Please.

SNAKE: He went that way. See the beach and beyond the beach. That wet stuff. Go fuck with that.

HARRY: It's cold.

SNAKE: Come on, it's time for your adventure. Come on, lie back down. You don't want to get these things wet. Wings for the snake man, wings for the snake. You get my drift? You should get so lucky, pal. If we're all the same then you realize that these are really my boots then. We've got good taste in boots . . .

He pulls off HARRY's *boots.*

Up now. Go get the wet, go.

HARRY *gets up holding his chest.*

HARRY: Pain here. Was that lightning?

SNAKE: Imagine that. Sheet lightning and no rain. And you can see the moon . . .

Picks up HARRY's *jacket. Puts it on himself.*

Thanks. No, really, I mean that.

HARRY: The moon.

SNAKE: Have you ever been there? Here, take some of this.

HARRY: Light.

SNAKE: Inhale. Hold.

HARRY: Ha. *(coughs)* I'm turning inside-out.

SNAKE: There you go, something's happening. See, that's unusual, not what you'd expect. You're having an experience. Something. Is this all you have? Nothing in your other pockets? See. The moon. We're there now. Christ, it's beautiful.

HARRY: The light.

SNAKE: You got a heart or something.

HARRY: Yes.

SNAKE: That doesn't work on the moon. Damn, look at that lightning. Come on, out you go. That's it.

HARRY: I can't see. Where are we?

SNAKE: Just walk forward. There. You didn't know that there was water on the moon did you?

HARRY: The water's cold.

SNAKE: Not much of an effort there, pal. The ocean looks pretty much the same, you didn't make much of an impression.

HARRY: I can see my child.

SNAKE: These boots of yours don't fit. Now, if we were really connected, the shoe should fit. You're just not paying attention, man.

LIGHTS: *Sheet lightning in the distance.*
SOUND: *After two seconds, distant thunder.*

HARRY: There was only one person born. We're all the same person.

SNAKE: I'll just have to get by. Wait, that open thing is happening.

HARRY: Help me out of the water. My hand. You don't need to be afraid.

SNAKE: It's her, she's coming.

HARRY: My son, you're my son.

SNAKE: Fuck you!

> *Stabs* HARRY *in his outstretched hand.* HARRY *puts his hand up to his mouth to taste his blood, then offers his hand to* SNAKE *again.*

Now that's disgusting. I warned you, I warned you . . . don't touch me, man . . .

> SNAKE *is unnerved. He runs from the scene shouting.*

Don't fuck with me, man . . . Don't you fuck with me.

> SNAKE *exits.* NURSE *and* ROBERT *enter and stand well behind* HARRY.

HARRY: The air and the water are becoming each other.

Oh, hello. Let me play a little while. Splish-splash in my bath. Hello, son. You're a good boy, my son, you are, you are . . . my son.

I see the whales, Robert . . .

They come dancing
Mother, Father dancing
Whales in the shadows
Swimming black

The Sound of Whales

> The whales in the hallway and I draw them
> With my blood I draw
> The sound, my God the sound . . .

The MUSIC *starts and* HARRY *talks in silence, miming to be heard. The* PIPES *are joined by* DRUMS. *He makes a gesture, trying to speak, and then is still. The* MUSIC *gets louder, the* DRUMS *in particular.* HARRY *is isolated by a* SINGLE LIGHT. *The* MUSIC *stops abruptly. One second of stillness.* BLACKOUT.

**DAVID MACLEAN** is an award-winning graphic designer, playwright and poet. **The Sound of Whales** was produced by Dark Horse Theatre in Vancouver in December, 1995. The impetus for **The Sound of Whales** came out of the author's (and his wife's) frustration dealing with the various bureaucracies regarding their son, who has Central Aphasia. Mr. MacLean lives in Deep Cove, B.C. with his wife, Jan, and their two children.

OTHER ANVIL DRAMA TITLES:

FRAGMENTS FROM THE BIG PIECE BY BRIAN KAUFMAN
ISBN: 1-895636-02-7; 44 PP; $6.95

SHYLOCK BY MARK LEIREN-YOUNG
ISBN: 1-895636-12-4; 64 PP; $9.95